SEASONAL PRAYER SERVICES FOR TEENAGERS

SEASONAL
PRAYER SERVICES
FOR
TEENAGERS

GREG DUES

XXIII

TWENTY-THIRD PUBLICATIONS
Mystic, Connecticut

Illustrations by William Baker

Twenty-Third Publications
P.O. Box 180
185 Willow Street
Mystic, CT 06355
(203) 536-2611

ISBN 0-89622-473-2
Library of Congress Catalog Card No. 90-71818

DEDICATION

To all the teenagers and youth ministers
who have shared their lives and prayer experiences with me
and especially to my two teenage daughters,
Elena and Francisca.

TABLE OF CONTENTS

Introduction..1

__CHAPTER__

1 AUTUMN:
Celebrating Transitions..5

2 HALLOWEEN:
Masks We Wear..8

3 HARVEST TIME:
The Miracle Of Seeds..12

4 ALL SOULS:
There's Life In Cemeteries..15

5 ADVENT:
Jesus Will Come Again..18

6 ADVENT:
Reconciliation Wreath...23

7 CHRISTMAS:
Celebrating Traditions...27

8 LENT:
Preparing A Contract..32

9 LENT:
Instruments Of Peace..35

10 THE TRIDUUM:
Signs Of New Life...40

11 EASTER:
An Emmaus Walk..47

12 PENTECOST:
Giving Witness...50

13 MAY:
A Testimony To Mary...54

14 THE SEASONS:
Celebrating Life's Cycles..57

15 SUNDAYS:
Why Go To Mass?..60

16 ALL YEAR:
Sharing Our Burdens..67

Reggie — may all your walking/journeys end at Emmaus!

Greg
7/24/91

SEASONAL PRAYER SERVICES FOR TEENAGERS

INTRODUCTION

We are Christians and we are on a journey of faith. Along the way we need to be cheered on and cheered up by other Christians. We need their spiritual support and we need to pray and worship with them. The teenagers in our churches need these things, too, probably even more than we adults do. That's the reason for this book.

These *Seasonal Prayer Services for Teenagers* evolved from actual "assemblies" I have coordinated over the years. They contain communal prayer and ritual especially geared to teenage interests and concerns, and I have written them all with what I call a "pep rally mentality." I have learned over the years that adolescents enjoy and learn best from events that encourage freedom of expression and individuality. A pep rally stirs up spirit, excitement, and promotes community identity, an *esprit de corps*. It calls for movement and encourages noise. I have therefore incorporated the dynamic of the pep rally in these services as much as possible.

I believe that effective religious assemblies can and do stir up spirit and excitement, and they can and do promote religious identity and community. What makes them effective is their acknowledgment that faith is something to get excited about. Our teenagers are moving forward with us on our journey of faith and this is worth celebrating. The activities and symbols we use with them should express our enthusiasm and joy. I have seen a great deal of enthusiasm and joy expressed during assemblies like these.

Why Ritual Is Important

Another necessary element for effective religious assemblies is ritual. Ritual is an established ceremonial form, even formal in ways, and it is intrinsic to any religious assembly. The best ritual will always draw people immediately to the ultimate purpose of the gathering. It will also offer them new ways to relate to one another and give them new structures for sharing what unites them.

Using ritual with our teenagers, however, does not mean that we have to subject them to highly stylized religious ceremonies. On the contrary, our assemblies with them can be informal and spontaneous and still incorporate ritualized patterns of religious behavior, as well as religious words, stories, and symbols. Bible readings, litanies, antiphonal prayers, bodily gestures, simple forms of dance, and choral readings are all examples of the kind of ritual I mean. And, the more these kinds of rituals reflect the real life experiences of teenagers, the more effective and attractive they will be.

By creating good assemblies that use good ritual, we will also be preparing our teenagers for greater participation in the church's eucharistic liturgy. According to the *Directory for Masses with Children*, "various kinds of celebrations" play a major role in the liturgical formation of young people and in their preparation for the church's liturgical life. By the very fact of celebration, they come to appreciate the liturgical elements of greeting, silence, and group prayer (paragraph #13).

Why Variety Is Important
The services in this book, while structured in similar ways, offer considerable variety, which is important when working with teenagers. To structure every prayer experience in exactly the same way, or to structure each as if it were a mini-Mass, is to be too predictable. (Remember that peprally mentality?) Thus, in this book, some of the services emphasize information or input from an adult leader. Others emphasize input from participants. Still others call for discussion and participation, and they all call for an active and enthusiastic response.

Keep in mind that the goal of these services is celebration. A healthy mix of listening, learning, and doing is important to keep the tone celebratory. An Advent service, for example, may require the sharing of information for participants to understand the season, but it should also include a way for them to actively and personally respond to God's Advent call.

The format of these services is also varied. In some, discussion comes first, then a response; in some the reading is from Scripture; in others the readings are produced by the participants themselves. An action or activity begins several of the services and reflection follows. Some of them are modeled directly on a pep rally, in which several sub-groups contribute separate pieces that build toward a particular goal or conclusion. (For example, one group might prepare a song, while another selects a reading. A third group might come up with a catchy refrain, and so on. All of these elements mix and mingle throughout the service.)

In a word, there is variety among these services, which adds the element of surprise. Surprise generates energy, excitement, and enthusiasm among teenagers, and that is my goal: to help teenagers get excited about and involved with God.

Service Components

Each of the services has the following components: *Background Notes, Preparation Instructions, Time to Listen* and *Response.* Though these four components are present in all, each service is nonetheless unique.

The *Background Notes* are intended to give youth ministers, catechists, and other presiders a sense of direction. They explain the purpose for the service and offer a brief catechetical rationale for celebrating it. The *Preparation* section gives specific directions about how to proceed and what materials to use. *Time to Listen* obviously involves listening to something; often the material is from Scripture, but not always. The *Response* section offers a concrete way for participants to react to what they have heard through discussion, prayer, and action.

Closing Thoughts

A good experience of prayer is obviously the goal of all these seasonal services. Although all the scripts offer one or more ways to pray, I encourage you to invite your teenagers to prepare some of the prayers themselves.

This adds a personal touch and creates a sense of ownership. You might also look for opportunities to encourage spontaneous prayer using prayer forms like general intercession, litanies, or antiphonal praying (as in the Litury of the Hours). All of the services in this book are meant to be adapted this way. No one resource can meet the particular needs of all youth programs everywhere. Indeed, no one resource can meet *your* particular and unique needs. It can only offer support. It's very important, then, that you adapt these services to the needs and circumstances of your particular group of teenagers.

Two additional resources that offer guidance in these directions are *Prayers for the Domestic Church: A Handbook for Worship in the Home* (Edward Hays, Hall Directory, Inc., Topeka, KS), and *Catholic Household Blessings and Prayers* (Bishop's Committee on the Liturgy, United States Catholic Conference, Washington, DC). Because both these resources are designed for home use, the wording is down to earth and practical.

May all of you who coordinate religious activities for adolescents: youth ministers, catechists, teachers, parents, DREs, principals, and pastors, pray often and well with your young people. May these *Seasonal Prayer Services for Teenagers* give you the courage and guidance you need to develop your own prayer experiences with and for your teenagers.

1
AUTUMN: CELEBRATING TRANSITIONS

Background Notes

This service celebrates the transition from one season to another. It focuses in particular on the transition teenagers make in autumn from the "lazy, hazy days of summer" to the routine of a new school year. Their clothes have changed. Their bodies have changed. Their fun and games have changed. Even their friends may have changed.

They are encouraged here to celebrate the wonder of an incarnate God who is present with them through all these transitions and changes. Christ walks with them as they adjust to new school experiences, re-adjust to old school friends and meet new ones, and experience the thrill of clubs, school games, and activities.

Preparation

Have available copies of Ecclesiastes 3:1-8 (as below). For variety and greater

involvement from participants, this reading has been divided into eight parts. Thus each reader proclaims the mystery of one particular "season" or phase of life. Those assigned to read should be given time to prepare.

Have available newsprint, chalkboard, or pieces of paper for the discussion segment.

Time to Listen
(Introduce this reading by explaining that it describes critical life phases and transitions.)

Reader One: There is a season for everything, a time for every concern under heaven.

Reader Two: There is a time for giving birth and a time for dying.

Reader Three: There is a time for planting and a time for uprooting what has been planted.

Reader Four: There is a time for killing and a time for healing; a time for knocking down and a time for building up.

Reader Five: There is a time for tears and a time for laughter; a time for mourning and a time for dancing.

Reader Six: There is a time for embracing and a time to refrain from embracing, a time for losing and a time for keeping.

Reader Seven: There is a time for keeping silent and a time for speaking.

Reader Eight: There is a time for loving and a time for hating; a time for war and a time for peace.

Reader One: There is a season for everything, a time for every concern under heaven.

Response
Using this Scripture text as a model, invite participants to first discuss the positive aspects—as well as challenges—of their summer experiences. Then ask: What are you experiencing now during the season of fall? What is this a "time" for? List their answers on newsprint or on a chalkboard where they are visible to all. (These answers will be used to help compose the concluding prayer liturgy.)

When all have contributed and the lists of transitions are complete, ask participants to gather in small groups to prepare the litany, using the observations that surfaced in the discussion. Offer the following as examples:

As we enjoy old friends and find new ones, we praise you, Lord.

As we remember July swimming and enjoy September football,
we praise you, Lord.

Closing Prayer
(Invite each small group to now pray its piece of the litany. Then, conclude
with the following blessing.)

Leader:
Lord of seasons, Lord of autumn,
We ask your blessing upon this wonderful time of year.
Bless our teachers and friends in school.
Bless our games, activities, and school work.
Bless our memories of summer.
Above all, bless this present moment
which is your gift to us.
We ask these things in the name of the Father
and of the Son and of the Holy Spirit.

All: Amen.

2
HALLOWEEN: MASKS WE WEAR

Background Notes

This assembly focuses on the masks and costumes people wear at Halloween. It also challenges the emotional patterns and "masks" that adolescents often assume for coping with personal growth and difficult situations at home and in school. Keep in mind that for teenagers a mask is more often a defense and survival technique than a sign of ill will.

This assembly challenges the false patterns of behavior teenagers adopt to impress peers or to avoid growing up. The leader should stress beforehand that the content is not intended to encourage "labeling" and is not directed personally toward any one in the group.

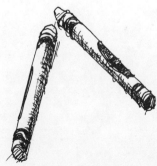

Preparation

Ask participants to divide into four groups. Provide each group with grocery bags, markers, crayons, and scissors from which a mask can be constructed. Assign one of these inscriptions to each group: "Better Than You," "The Cool One," "Wishy-Washy," "Born Loser," and "Ever Popular." Give each group a written description of its "character" (as below), and ask them to cut out and decorate the masks.

Invite participants to discuss these descriptions as they work on their masks and to adapt them to fit their own experiences. Each group should pick a representative who will practice and then read its description at the appropriate time during this service.

Time to Listen

Leader: A reading from the letter to the Corinthians (2 Cor 4, 1-6, adapted):
God has called us to the work of the Gospel, so we should not get discouraged. Rather, we should put aside all secret and shameful deeds; we should not act with deceit or try to cover up the truth. In the full light of truth we should live in God's sight and try to help others do the same.

This is the Word of the Lord.

All: Thanks be to God.

(As the following readings begin, one volunteer from each group should wear the mask being described. Mask-wearers should sit with their backs to the assembly. As each mask is described, the wearer should turn and face the group.)

Reader One: Masks. When we hear this word, most of us probably think of disguises that hide our faces on Halloween. Some are scary, grotesque, monster-like. Others are cheery, smiling, clown-like. Such masks help us create an image of what we ordinarily are not.

Reader Two: There's another kind of mask we sometimes hide behind. Others don't see it, but we know it's there. We keep our real selves behind it. We're afraid to let people know who we really are, so we "mask" ourselves. Others might not like the "real" us. They might not want to be our friend. We would be left alone, and that's scary.

Right now we're going to reveal four different masks that we sometimes wear. We're not making fun of these behaviors; we're simply offering them as a subject for your personal reflection.

Better-Than-You: I am "better-than-you." I hide behind whatever makes me look better than others. I don't have too many real friends because they might tell me things about myself that I don't want to hear. I avoid ordinary people because they might bring me down to their level. My goal is to stay "one-up" on everyone else.

The Cool One: I am "the cool one." I always dress great and I always do the "right thing," the things popular people do. I hang out with the "in" crowd, even when I don't enjoy what's going on. I don't have to enjoy it, I just have to be there because that's what counts.

Wishy-Washy: My name is "wishy-washy." I agree with whatever those around me say or do. I never express my own opinion because I don't have one. I do whatever other people tell me, and I say whatever I'm supposed to say to please them. Tomorrow I'll probably do and say something different. I never take a stand on anything.

The Born Loser: I am "the born loser." Everything, and I repeat, everything seems to go wrong for me. I can study all night for a test and still not get a good grade. Other people think they have it bad, but I have it worse. I don't have as many opportunities and privileges as other kids do. Everybody else has lots more friends than I do. Nobody has it as bad as I do.

Ever Popular: You can call me "ever popular." Everybody thinks I'm great. I know almost everyone, but I don't have time for close friends, ones I can really trust. I don't have time to go beneath the surface with people. But that's okay. My motto is: "It's the quantity of friends that counts!"

Reader Three: Getting rid of a mask is not easy. First we have to look inside ourselves to see who and what we really are. We have to believe in our own goodness and in the gifts God has given us. We have to believe that we are okay just as we are. Only then can others accept us for who we really are. It takes real courage and effort to let people know us this way, but with God's help we can do it.

Response

Lead participants in an "unmasking" ritual in the following way. First introduce a period of silent reflection and prayer. During this silence, invite participants to think about a time when they tried to be someone else. Use these or similar questions: Why did you want to appear to be someone you weren't? What did you do that was unusual behavior for you? Have you ever worn any of the masks we have just described?

After this reflection invite those volunteers wearing the paper-bag masks to take them off one at a time. In turn, each should say: "I am not (name of mask). I am (name), and I'm okay the way I am." When each wearer has spoken, take all the masks, tear them up and dramatically throw them away. If your setting allows, you might even burn the masks.

Closing Prayer

Leader: God, our loving parent, you have made each of us unique. You have given us unique personalities and special gifts and talents. Help us to be proud of who we are. Forgive us when we try to be someone else in order to please others. Teach us how to take off our masks. We ask these things in the name of the Father and of the Son and of the Holy Spirit.

All: Amen.

3
HARVEST TIME: THE MIRACLE OF SEEDS

Background Notes

This is the time of year when trees and plants, so vibrant in spring and summer, prepare to die. But they do so in a blaze of glory!

Many of the harvest things we see, touch, and eat are full of seeds: pumpkins, squash, and apples, for example. Other harvest things actually *are* seeds: wheat, corn, and other grains harvested in late summer. There is mystery and new life in these seeds. They are an aspect of God's continuing creative action.

The dying associated with autumn actually produces a harvest that is necessary for our living. Seeds are an essential part of our diet, for example, the breads and cereals made from wheat, corn, oats, and nuts. Some become the diet for animals and birds. Others, with the miracle of new life within them, generate new plants in the spring.

Many young people, because of their urban environment, haven't had the

opportunity to experience the cycle of planting, growing, and harvesting. It might help if before the assembly, you review with them the cycle of life that all seeds go through.

Planting, of course, is ordinarily associated with springtime. During autumn, however, seeds from perennial flowers (whose summer beauty has faded) and from some fruits and vegetables, fall to the ground. Many trees drop their seeds in summer, and in fall cover them over with a protective blanket of leaves.

Optional: Arrange to take your teenagers on a field trip to a local produce market, one filled with harvest foods, or at least to the produce section of a local supermarket. Precede the field trip with the discussion mentioned above.

Preparation

Ask for volunteers to decorate your assembly area with a harvest theme. Emphasize food stuffs that actually are seeds or that have seeds within them. If this service is celebrated close to Thanksgiving, decorations from this holiday might also be included or featured.

Time to Listen

Reader: In John 12:24, Jesus speaks about a kind of dying that produces new life. This is what he says, "Amen, amen, I say to you, unless a grain of wheat falls to the ground and dies, it remains just a grain of wheat; but if it dies, it produces much fruit."

This is the Word of the Lord.

All: Thanks be to God.

Response

After this simple Scripture proclamation, discuss with participants the mystery of continuing creation in the cycle of life. (See the Background Notes above.) There is always the potency (seed) for new life in nature. Keep a record of things your young people contribute to this discussion for possible re-use during the following "Thanksgiving Litany."

To prepare invocations for the litany, ask participants to form in groups of two or three and prepare a list of harvest gifts for which they are grateful. Offer suggestions based on your earlier discussion. Once their list is complete, ask them to write out invocations. Have every person present pray at least

one invocation during the litany.
Explain that you will be pausing
between each invocation for personal silent prayer.

Sample Invocations

• For the seeds that become our bread
and cereal, we thank you, God of the
harvest...

(pause)

• For the seeds that become new life, we thank you, God of the harvest...

(pause)

• For ripe tomatoes, we thank you, God of the harvest...

(pause)

• For the mystery of dying from which life emerges, we thank you, God of the
harvest...

(Pause, and then invite participants to pray their own invocations.)

Closing Prayer

Leader:

God of seasons, God of the harvest,
we ask your blessing upon the harvest
that is now beginning to accumulate
in our barns and produce markets.
God of seasons, God of the harvest,
thank you for these foods.
We will eat them with gratitude
and share them with love.
We ask these things in the name of the Father
and of the Son and of the Holy Spirit.

All: Amen.

4
ALL SOULS: THERE'S LIFE IN CEMETERIES

Background Notes

The most memorable assembly I ever coordinated took place on a parish bus parked in a cemetery. After the bus arrived, I shared a brief message about death with the young people as they looked out the windows at the graves all around them. I referred to the life-cycle theme (developed in the preceding service), and I offered positive insights into the cycle of life-death-life by focusing on the cycle of seasons and harvest time.

Preparation

Arrange for a field trip to a local cemetery, preferably one that has some association with your parish and your particular group.

Assign readers for the Scripture passages (as below). Encourage readers to proclaim them clearly and dramatically.

Make a list of parishioners who are buried in the cemetery. Ahead of time, scout out the locations of some of these graves. Or, list any other graves you or your group might want to visit.

Prepare a litany from your list and include in the litany any well-known people (national celebrities), who have recently died. Take this list with you to the cemetery.

Time to Listen

Once you arrive at the cemetery, invite the readers to make this Scripture proclamation from Thessalonians 5, 4-25 (adapted).

Reader One: Brothers and sisters, we are not in darkness, so the day of death will not overtake us like a thief. We are not people of the night, but rather we are children of the light and children of the day. Because we live in the light, death should not be a threat to us.

Reader Two: God did not destine us for evil and punishment, but to gain salvation through Jesus Christ who died for us that we might have life. In life and in death we live in the presence of Jesus. So, let us encourage one another and build one another up in all that we do.

Reader Three: May the God of peace make you perfectly holy and may you be preserved entirely: spirit, soul, and body, for the coming of our Lord, Jesus Christ.

This is the Word of the Lord.

All: Thanks be to God.

Response

Invite participants to spend time freely roaming around the cemetery visiting the graves of loved ones, looking for the oldest grave, etc. Show them how to make rubbings (with colored chalk or crayons on paper overlaying the grave marker).

While still among the graves, again assemble your group and invite them to share their experiences and feelings about death, including what they have experienced today. How do they feel about death now? What does their faith tell them about death and what comes after? What questions do they have about this experience.

Finally, pray a litany with the list you and your group prepared ahead of time, using this or a similar pattern:

Leader: Let us remember (name) who was born (date) and who died on (date). May he (she) rest in peace.

All: Thank you, God, for memories of this person.
(Continue until you have covered all the names on your list, and then conclude with the closing prayer.)

Closing Prayer

Leader: Eternal rest grant unto them, O Lord.

All: And let perpetual light shine upon them.

Leader: May they rest in peace.

All: Amen.

Leader: May their souls and the souls of all the faithful departed, through the mercy of God, rest in peace.

All: Amen.

Optional Activities

If a trip to a cemetery is not possible, invite a speaker (perhaps someone from the diocese or a member of your parish staff) to talk to your group about the natural cycles of life and death, using nature as an example of God's plan for all living things.

A second option is to invite your parish liturgist and/or pastor to discuss parish customs regarding wakes and funerals, stressing Christian teachings about life after death.

5
ADVENT: JESUS WILL COME AGAIN

Background Notes

Exciting things are happening at this time of year. Little children, as well as adolescents and adults, are excited about Bethlehem, the infant Jesus, and Santa Claus. Red and green Christmas colors perk up the winter dullness. This is a wonderful time of year. It's also Advent!

We know there's more to Advent than the excitement generated by external signs. Advent invites us inward as well, to think about the presence of Jesus: his coming every day into our lives and his final coming at the end of time. Adolescents can be challenged to prepare for these comings.

The liturgical season of Advent creates a sort of thematic tension. The penitential color of purple clashes with the more joyful Christmas colors. (However, dark blue, an ancient Advent color, is once again becoming popular.) Lights on the Advent Wreath challenge the twinkling of Christmas lights in windows and on trees. Our parish Advent reconciliation services are scheduled on calendars filled with Christmas preparations.

Note: This assembly is an example of a rally assembly, described in the Introduction as one that pulls together many different pieces, contributed by separate groups who have prepared and rehearsed only their own piece. This assembly can, however, also be celebrated effectively by a single group, and would be a good service for family groups.

Preparation

Divide participants by "lot" into two groups: "believers" and "unbelievers." These groups will do a choral recitation that forms the heart of this service.

Explain beforehand that this is an artificial or contrived labeling.

Choral recitations are most effective when done in a formal manner. For this service then "believers" and "unbelievers" should stand facing each other, possibly from opposite sides of the assembly area. Rehearse with each group ahead of time so that parts will be read clearly, dramatically, and with enthusiasm.

Time to Listen

Leader: God speaks to us in the Bible through the prophets who proclaimed the coming and continuing presence of the Messiah. In the following recitation we will hear the words of the prophets echoed. Let us listen with our minds and hearts.

Believers: Our Lord will come again!
Our Lord will come again!

Unbelievers: What is this you say?
"Our Lord will come again?"
Who is this Lord?

Believers: Our Lord who was a carpenter, is now our savior, and our brother.
He lives with us.
He teaches us and he heals us.
He takes away our sins,
and shows us the way to live.
He dwells now with God
but he will come again.

Unbelievers: What is this you say?
Where is this Lord?
How do you know that he will come again?
What is this you say?

Believers: We know that he will come again
because he has promised it!
Even now when we gather in his name, he is among us
through the Holy Spirit, his gift to us.
His presence makes us happy.
His presence saves us!
We shout for joy!

Unbelievers: What is this you say?
Why should you sing and dance,
and shout for joy?
What is this you say?

Believers: We rejoice because Jesus will come again.
In truth he is already here
through his spirit of peace and joy.
He is here with us!
We have his love. He is here!
We follow his way. He is here!
We sing and we dance
and we shout for joy!
He will come again! He is here!

Unbelievers: We do not believe you!
We do not believe you!
We know you. We know you.
You are not what you say you are!
Look and listen! Look and listen!

First Speaker: (A representative of the "unbelievers" steps forward and speaks:) Your savior's birth was announced at Bethlehem with these words: "Peace on earth." But where is this peace?
Is it in your homes, your schools, among your friends? I see you cutting down your

parents and friends. I see your fighting and your jealousy. And look at our world. Children are suffering and starving. And you don't seem to care. People are poor, and sick, and lonely. Jesus promised peace, but you don't give it. We unbelievers look at you and wonder....

Optional Slide Presentation

If possible, pause at this point for a silent slide meditation. Choose slides that show poverty and suffering. If slides are not available or convenient, silently hold up pictures and headlines from newspapers and magazines that reveal suffering. Then continue as follows.

Believers: No! No! No! Look more carefully!
You will see our love and goodness.
You will see the Lord present in what we do.
Look! Look! Look!

Second Speaker: (A representative of the "believers" steps forward and speaks:) Jesus still stretches out his hands to touch people through our hands. Though we sometimes fail, we do make an effort to love our parents and friends. We do try to offer peace. Many Christians are trying to offer healing to those who suffer. They do feed the hungry. They do hold the hands of the lonely. They do share what they have with the poor.

We are trying to offer peace on earth.

Believers: We are weak at times, but we do try.

This is why we wait
for Jesus to come again.
He will strengthen us.
He will touch us with peace and love.
He will forgive us and teach us how to forgive.

Unbelievers: We shall see! We shall see!
Show us how to believe.
Show us who this Jesus is.
Show us by the way you live.

Response and Closing Prayer

Invite "believers" and "unbelievers" to meld into one large group. Then pray the following prayer slowly and dramatically.

Leader: Lord God our Father,
We pray to you in the name of Jesus.
We pray as your children.

Speaker One: You sent Jesus to us and he saved us.
But we do not always live as saved people.
Sometimes there is little difference
between us and the unbelievers.

Speaker Two: Help us to live the peace that Jesus brought us.
Help us to walk the way that he showed us.
Help us to be as loving and as unselfish as he was.

Leader: Father, when we are weak, make us strong in faith and action. Take away our sin as we wait for Jesus to come again. As we wait for Christmas, we promise to change and grow as believers. We ask these things through Jesus, your Son.

All: Amen.

6
ADVENT : RECONCILIATION WREATH

Background Notes

Lighting an Advent wreath is a popular tradition that began in Germany. Like other popular Advent customs, it came to this country in the mid to late 1800s with immigrants.

The Advent wreath celebrates the tension between dark and light as the winter solstice approaches. It serves as a symbol for the tension between the spiritual darkness of sin and the light of salvation, a light that began with the birth of Jesus. "The light shines on in the darkness, and the darkness did not overcome it" (John 2:5).

Each week one more candle is lit. The light grows more brightly. The coming of Jesus is getting closer. "For our salvation is nearer now than when we first believed; the night is advanced, the day is at hand. Let us throw off the works of darkness and put on the armor of light" (Romans 13:11-12).

For this service, the Advent wreath is used as a centering symbol that promotes reconciliation and transformation in preparation for the coming of Jesus. This is a departure from the traditional symbolism of the Advent wreath. Here each candle will be symbolic of one area of a teenager's life: home, school, parish, and within the peer group.

This service can be followed by the sacrament of reconciliation, if so desired.

Preparation

Prepare four blank Christmas cards (preferably homemade ones) for each participant. These will be used during the concluding absolution.

If possible, darken the assembly area. Place a large Advent wreath in a prominent place. Make sure the four candles can be easily lit. Matches and a taper should be in an obvious place.

Time to Listen

Reader One: A reading from the prophet Isaiah:
The people who walked in darkness have seen a great light; upon those who dwelt in the land of gloom a light has shone.

Reader Two: They lived in the land of shadows, but now a light is shining on them. You have given them great joy, Lord, you have made them happy."
rd of the Lord.

All: Thanks be to God.

Response

Reader One: Jesus Christ is with us in our homes as we live, work, and play with our families. However, we often ignore this presence of Christ in our homes. We aggravate our parents, who are already burdened with work and stress. We resist doing our share of family chores. We make brothers and sisters unhappy. We choose to live in the darkness.

(The first candle is blown out.)

Leader: Let us pause and think about the ways we have sinned at home.

(Pause for one minute then re-light the first candle. Ask participants to repeat the following refrain after you: Come, Lord Jesus, burn brightly during the hours I spend at home with my family.)

All: Come, Lord Jesus, burn brightly during the hours I spend at home with my family.

(The second candle is lit.)

Reader Two: Jesus Christ is with us at school and during all after-school activities. He is in our classrooms, hallways, and lunchrooms. However, we tend to ignore this presence of Christ in the way we behave. We live, study, work, and play as though Jesus Christ makes no difference in our school life. We choose to live in the dark.

(The candle is blown out.)

Leader: Let us pause and think about the ways we have sinned during school hours.

(Pause for one minute and then re-light the candle.)

Repeat after me: "Come, Lord Jesus, burn brightly during my school hours."

All: Come, Lord Jesus, burn brightly during my school hours.

(The third candle is lit.)

Reader Three: Jesus Christ is with us in our parish as we come together to pray, worship, and grow in faith. However, we often ignore this presence of Christ, not listening to the word of Scripture when it is read and preached. We sometimes refuse to go to church or complain loudly about going. We do not pray. We refuse to give our time to parish youth activities. We do not want to hear about our Gospel responsibility to feed the hungry and serve the poor. We choose to live in the darkness.

(The third candle is blown out.)

Leader: Let us pause and evaluate the way we spend our time here at the parish, especially at liturgy.

(Pause for one minute and then re-light the third candle, saying: Come, Lord Jesus, burn brightly while I pray, worship, and search for a better relationship with you.)

All: Come, Lord Jesus, burn brightly while I pray, worship, and search for a better relationship with you.

(The fourth and final candle is lit.)

Reader Four: Jesus Christ is with us whenever we spend time with our friends. We often ignore this presence of Christ in the things we do and the way we talk. We pick and choose our friends on the basis of popularity. We gossip. We use people. We act as though Jesus Christ makes no difference to us and our friends. We choose to live in darkness.

(The candle is blown out.)

Leader: Let us pause and think about the ways we sin when we are with our friends.

(Pause for one minute and then re-light candle four, while saying: Come, Lord Jesus, burn brightly while I am with my friends.)

All: Come, Lord Jesus, burn brightly while I am with my friends.
(Now give each participant four blank Christmas cards. Invite them to write a Christmas message to four people, one from home, one from school, one from the parish, and one from their peer group, with whom they need to be reconciled. For example: At home it could be a parent or sibling; at school a teacher or classmate; in the parish, the priest or youth minister; among friends, anyone they have hurt or been hurt by.

(Invite participants to take the cards home with them as a reminder of their need for reconciliation, and when they feel able to do so, to actually give the cards to the persons involved.)

Closing Prayer

Leader: Come, Lord Jesus, be with us at home and be with us at school. Teach us to acknowledge your presence when we gather in our parish to pray and worship. Most of all, teach us to be aware of your presence among our friends. You are our best and most faithful friend. Show us how to return your love. We ask you these things in the name of the Father and of the Son and of the Holy Spirit.

All: Amen.

7
CHRISTMAS: CELEBRATING TRADITIONS

Background Notes

Everywhere we look, everywhere we go, exciting things are happening this time of year. Colored lights twinkle where just weeks ago there was darkness. Seasonal music replaces the usual musak. Something is about to happen, and waiting for it feels good.

This assembly is designed to be celebrated with families. The location should be a multipurpose room or hall where families can gather comfortably, preferably around tables.

It focuses on popular Christmas traditions, providing a sort of seasonal smorgasboard. "Readers" provide important pieces of information. The readings are followed by simple family rituals that participants should be encouraged to duplicate in their homes.

Preparation

Ahead of time communicate with families, asking them to bring to the assembly an ornament from their family Christmas tree and a figurine from their family nativity creche. (These will be returned immediately after the assembly.) Also ask each family to bring a refreshment for sharing during the party.

The following "props" should be in a prominent place so that all are able to see them at the proper time: a Christmas tree, a table for the nativity figurines, and a large bunch of mistletoe.

Also ahead of time, have the young people prepare two giant Christmas cards from packing box cardboard: "A Christmas Card to the World" and "A Christmas Card to the Parish." Have them write in with markers what they wish for the world and the parish at this time of year. These cards should also be set up in your assembly area.

Duplicate the special blessing and prayer cards that will be used by the families during the assembly (see directions below). Finally, practice with the Announcer and the Readers beforehand.

Time to Listen

Begin this assembly with a family table activity of listening and sharing. Invite families to discuss their Christmas traditions with the other families at their table using these starters:

1) What are your favorite traditions?

2) What do these traditions mean to the various members of your family, to grandparents, parents, teens, children, neighbors, community?

3) How would you feel if these traditions were lost?

Allow ten minutes or so for this sharing. Then continue as below.

Announcer: Our first custom this evening is called "A Light In The Dark."

(Turn out or lower the lights.)

Reader One: Feel the dark, imagine the cold. This is the time of year when nights are long and days are short. Many of our Christmas traditions come from Northern Europe, especially Germany, where cold and dark are predominant.

Reader Two: In ancient times, German families would burn special lights in their huts and homes. These lights offered cheer and warmth in a world of darkness and cold. Families would bring evergreen branches indoors as a reminder that green things would grow again. These green branches were a sign of hope.

Reader Three: When these people became Christians, their popular winter customs took on new meaning. Now they celebrated the birth of Jesus who is the light of the world. The winter lights celebrated by pagans became Christmas lights celebrated by Christians. Their special evergreens became symbols of hope and anticipation for the coming of the Messiah.

Response

Pray together the following blessing, using the prayer cards at each table.

Leader: Let us pray. Jesus, you are the light of the world.

All: Jesus, you are the light of the world.

Leader: Teach us how to live in your light.

All: Teach us how to live in your light.

Leader: May the darkness of sin never touch our lives.

All: May the darkness of sin never touch our lives.

Leader: We ask these things in the name of the Father and of the Son and of the Holy Spirit.

All: Amen.

(Lights can be turned back on.)

Announcer: Our second custom is "The Story of the Christmas Tree."

Reader Four: In ancient times Christians celebrated the feast of Adam and Eve on December 24. They staged a play about the garden of paradise and the biblical story of creation. On the stage was a "Paradise Tree" with fruit hanging on it, usually apples. Children liked the story and the tree. They begged their parents to put up "Paradise Trees" at home.

Reader Five: The burning of special winter lights was a popular pagan custom. Soon these special winter lights were put on the "Paradise Tree." This is how the custom of having a Christmas tree began. The green branches remind us to have hope, and the lights remind us of the coming of Jesus, who is the light of the world. The ornaments are the "fruits of paradise" that Jesus offers us.

Response

(Invite families to come forward to place their ornaments on the tree. Then pray together the following blessing using the prayer cards at each table.)

Leader: God of life and light, we ask your blessing upon this tree.

All: Bless these ornaments that come from our own family trees.

Leader: May this tree's green branches be a sign of the hope that Jesus gives.

All: May these glittering ornaments be a sign of the joy we share with our families.

Leader: May the gifts beneath our trees on Christmas Day be signs of our love and care for one another.

Announcer: Our third custom is "The Story of Mistletoe."

Reader Six: Mistletoe is a parasite that grows on oak trees in some parts of the world. In ancient times mistletoe was considered a magical plant with healing powers. It was gathered by pagan priests in a sacred ceremony. Each family would take a piece to hang over its door. There it was supposed to protect and heal everyone in the house.

Reader Seven: When enemies met under the sacred mistletoe in the forest, they would put away their weapons and offer one another signs of friendship. Eventually, especially in England, this healing mistletoe became a symbol of Christ, the divine healer. Today, however, it is more a sign of merriment, and the custom is that when people meet under the mistletoe, they kiss.

Response

Invite participants to now share a sign of love, healing, and reconciliation. If possible, have pieces of mistletoe at each table.

Announcer: Our fourth custom is "The Story of the Creche."

Reader Eight: Tradition has it that Jesus was born outside the town of Bethlehem in a stable or cave. His first visitors were shepherds and their animals, especially sheep and goats. Almost 900 years ago, Francis of Assisi looked for a way to remind people that Jesus was born in a lonely stable. He prepared a Christmas tableau that told the story of Jesus' birth, using real people and live animals.

Reader Nine: In this way a popular Christmas custom began. People began to prepare little figures of the people and animals that were part of the Bethlehem scene. Today many Christian homes have a Christmas stable with statues of Mary, Joseph, Jesus in the manger, shepherds, and animals. A Nativity set is also called a *creche*, which is French for crib.

Response

Invite families to bring forward their figurines and place them on the table prepared for this purpose. Then invite all present to pray the following blessing (from the prayer card at their tables).

Leader: God of love, bless these nativity figurines.

All: They will be part of the Christmas Nativity scene in our homes.

Leader: May they remind us of the birth of your son, Jesus. May they remind us of the poverty in which Jesus was born.

All: May they remind us to reach out to the poor and the homeless among us. Amen.

Closing Testimony

Invite representatives from among the young people to come forward and explain the messages contained within their giant Christmas cards. Then conclude with a party.

8
LENT:
PREPARING
A CONTRACT

Background Notes

The liturgical season of Lent is celebrated within the church as a six-week spiritual journey. It begins on Ash Wednesday and moves steadily toward personal and community resurrection at Eastertime. For some catechumens in the parish, this journey leads to baptism. For others it leads to full membership in the Catholic Church.

The season of Lent parallels the dramatic changes taking place in nature. The word itself hints at this. "Lent" comes from the Anglo Saxon *lencten* or "lengthening," and is the equivalent of our word springtime. It describes the gradual lengthening of the hours of daylight, which produce a new warming and the first hints of new growth. This warming trend is more or less obvious, depending on when Lent begins and geographic location.

During Lent we Christians journey symbolically from spiritual coldness and sin to the warmth of forgiveness and new life at Easter. This assembly focuses on an aspect of this journey: the signing of a personal lenten contract (as below) that calls for prayer, fasting and abstinence, and good works.

Preparation

Invite your young people to decorate your assembly area to show the contrast between winter and spring. They can use pictures and posters, weather forecasts from the local paper (enlarged on a copier), snowflakes, flowers and butterflies, etc. Encourage creativity.

Prepare the contract forms (as below) ahead of time, adapting the suggested content to your own group. Also, set up a table beneath a cross or prepare a large cross to which items can be tacked.

Time to Listen

Reader: A reading from Paul's letter to the Ephesians (Chapter 5: 8-16): There was a time when you were in darkness, but now you are light in the Lord. Well, then, live as children of light. Light produces every kind of goodness and justice and truth. Be correct in your judgment of what pleases the Lord. Take no part in vain deeds done in darkness; rather condemn them. Keep careful watch over your conduct. Do not act like fools, but like thoughtful people. Make the most of the present opportunity, for these are evil days.

This is the Word of the Lord.

All: Thanks be to God.

Response

Now invite participants to discuss and fill in lenten contracts with these or similar words on them.

I, _____, am beginning my lenten journey. I recognize that I often yield to the spiritual coldness of sin in these ways:
(Check off appropriate items. Add any not listed.)

____my tendency toward angry silence

____my lack of communication

____my selfishness

____my hurting words

____my habits and addictions

I resolve to move toward the new life of Easter as follows:

•ways I will pray:

_____
_____

_____

•ways I will fast and abstain:

_____
_____
_____

•good works I will do:

_____
_____
_____

When I arrive at Easter I hope to see the following changes:

_____
_____

_____

I hereby sign my name to this lenten contract.

Signed:_____

(When the contracts are completed, invite participants to put them in envelopes and then come forward to place them on the table beneath the cross. Or, have them tack their contracts to the large cross you have prepared.)

Closing Prayer

Leader: Jesus, during these weeks of Lent, we walk with you and you walk with us. Stay close to us so that through your warmth the winter cold of our sins might be replaced. May we share in your new life when we arrive together at Easter. We ask these things in the name of the Father and of the Son and of the Holy Spirit.

All: Amen.

9
LENT: INSTRUMENTS OF PEACE

Background Notes

The theme of this assembly (based on the popular prayer of Francis of Assisi) is "Make Me an Instrument of Your Peace." Because Lent is the season of conversion, this is a particularly apt theme for this time in the liturgical year.

Lent comes in springtime, a time when darkness and cold are no longer as severe as in winter. This transition in nature is symbolic of our own transition out of the dark and cold of hatred, injury, doubt, despair, and sadness into the joy and light of Easter. The prayer of Saint Francis highlights this transition. In it we pray for the grace to move from experiences of sin and spiritual darkness to the wonders of grace and light.

Note: Because of this dark/light theme, this assembly, with some adjustments, might also be very appropriate for Advent when Isaiah proclaims: "The people who walked in darkness have seen a great light; upon those who dwelt in the land of gloom a light has shone" (Isaiah 9:1).

Because of the "confessions" in the choral readings and the proclamations of absolution, you might want to use this service in preparation for the sacrament of reconciliation. And, because this service is particularly long, you might want to divide it and use it during several lenten sessions.

Preparation

Beforehand, invite your young people to write down experiences they or their peers have had of hatred, injury, doubt, despair, sadness, and darkness. Then ask them to contrast these with their experiences of love, pardon, faith, hope, joy, and light. As they recall their experiences, can they feel or imagine the transition or movement from the "dark side" to the "light side"? Explain that this service will focus on this transition.

Time to Listen:

Leader: Let this prayer be the word God speaks to us today.
Please repeat each line after me.

Lord, make me an instrument of your peace.
Where there is hatred, let me sow love;
Where there is injury, pardon;
Where there is doubt, faith;
Where there is despair, hope;
Where there is sadness, joy;
Where there is darkness, light.
O Divine Master, grant that I may not
So much seek to be consoled, as to console.
Not so much to be understood as to understand.
Not so much to be loved, as to love.
For it is in giving that we receive.
It is in pardoning that we are pardoned.
It is in dying that we are born to eternal life.
Amen.

Response: Confession of Hatred and Injury

(Suggest that while participants are reciting these lines one person in the group should step forward to perform a bodily gesture that suggests being bound or shackled, for example, by tightly balling his or her fists or arms.)

All: Shackled. Shackled.
Who will break our chains?

Left: We are shackled by our hatred.
We hand-pick our friends.

Right: We avoid those who are different,
those who remind us that we are not perfect.

Left: We separate others on the basis of money and clothes
and the color of their skin.

Right: Our hatred sometimes turns to fear.
What if those who are different overpower us?

Left: Our hatred allows us to injure them
through insinuation, lies, and gossip.

Right: And so we shun them in our school halls
and even in our churches.

All: Shackled. Shackled.
Who will break our chains?

Reader One: 1 Corinthians 13: 1-13

Leader: The chains of hatred and injury can be broken only with love and pardon. The grace for both is available to us. Let us offer them in practical ways, with apologies and promises, with honest statements and humble explanations, with open arms and hugs. Let us be instruments of love and pardon by defending the innocent, supporting the weak, understanding the misunderstood. Little by little, day by day, let us become givers of love and pardon.

Response 2: Confession of Doubt and Despair
(Ask one of the participants to assume a bodily gesture that symbolizes despair, for example a bowed head.)

All: What's the use! What's the use!
Is life worth living? Is God worth believing?

Left: My friends don't believe me,
My parents don't trust me,
And nobody listens to me.

Right: My friends depress me with their problems,
but I have problems of my own—and no answers.

Left: There are things I want so badly,
but I just don't seem to get them.

Right: Life is so short—and it seems to be getting shorter.

It's so empty, and it has no meaning.

Left: There are disasters of nature, and sickness of body.
There are broken loves, and there is death.

Right: I feel so worthless. I am such a failure,
nobody seems to care.

Left: My parents demand that I be what I am not.
Then they disappear when I need them.

Right: Even God doesn't care.
I don't see proof of it in my life.

All: What's the use! What's the use!
Is life worth living? Is God worth believing?

Reader Three: Psalm 96:1-13

Reader Four: Trust in surprises and you will find faith and hope. God is a surprise, always holding out new possibilities. Watch for the signs. Just when everything seems at it's worst, there will be a surprise. It can come from a friend, or a stranger. It can come from Scripture, from a book, or TV. And, what you hope to receive from others, also give. Be there for others. Surprise them. When you trust in God and think of others, then you will find faith and hope.

Response 3: Confession of Sadness and Darkness
(Invite one of the participants to assume a bodily gesture of sadness, perhaps by holding his or her arms limply or by making a sad face.)

All: The world is so dark, and life is so sad.
    Where is the sunrise? Where is the sunrise?

Right: I failed another test, I didn't finish my homework.
    What's the use of learning worthless things anyway?

Left: Parents and teachers smother and protect me,
    But they reject me when I need them.

Right: I get angry words and violations of love,
    from those who claim to be my friends.

Left: Everyone else is so popular,
    But no one chooses me.

Right: I am tempted to look for light in drugs and alcohol
    But I'm afraid I'll only find deeper darkness.

Left: I am tempted to go after shallow sexual friendships,
But I'm afraid I'll only find deeper sadness.

All: The world is so dark, and life is so sad.
Where is the sunrise? Where is the sunrise?

Reader Five: John 8:12

Reader Six: Someone once said: "If you make a mountain out of a molehill, don't expect anyone to climb up and enjoy the view!" There is the possibility of joy within us. Let us find it. There is a light inside us. Let us turn it on! We will find joy and walk in the light only if we crawl out of the dark and enjoy others. Let us reach out and make someone else happy and then we'll be happy. Let us walk in the light and then our lives will be bright. Let us remember that we are not alone. The light of the world, Jesus, is always with us. Let us rejoice and be glad.

Closing Prayer

Leader: Let us now offer one another a sign of peace. (When all have extended peace, close as you began, with the Prayer of Saint Francis. Ask participants to again repeat each line after you.)

> Lord, make me an instrument of your peace.
> Where there is hatred, let me sow love;
> Where there is injury, pardon;
> Where there is doubt, faith;
> Where there is despair, hope;
> Where there is sadness, joy;
> Where there is darkness, light.
> O Divine Master, grant that I may not
> So much seek to be consoled,
> As to console, not so much to be understood
> As to understand; not so much to be loved,
> As to love.
> For it is in giving that we receive,
> It is in pardoning that we are pardoned.
> It is in dying that we are born to eternal life.
> Amen.

10

THE TRIDUUM: SIGNS OF NEW LIFE

Background Notes

Holy Week is the "week of weeks" for Christians. During it we focus on the death and resurrection of Jesus. There would be no Christianity without the events we commemorate during this week. There would be no Christian churches. Without this week, there would be no Christ the Lord!

Holy Week, as we celebrate it today, began in the City of Jerusalem. It was there that Jesus suffered, died, and was raised from the dead. The followers of Jesus wanted to re-live those important moments. They believed that Jesus would be with them as they did so. Through ritual and story they retold and experienced anew the story of salvation.

Every year the church retells this holy story through ritual and the Word of Scripture. What happened two thousand years ago is present again each time these great mysteries are commemorated.

Unfortunately, not that many teenagers experience the great mysteries celebrated during the Triduum (the "three days" of Holy Thursday, Good Friday, and Holy Saturday/Easter Vigil). Consequently, they never learn about some of the fundamental symbols of Christianity. The purpose of this assembly then is to explain and celebrate these mysteries by directing attention to the rich and sensual symbolism of the Sacred Triduum.

Again, because of length, you might decide to divide this material and use it in several sessions. Ideally, however, the assembly should take place just before Holy Week.

Preparation

As with all gatherings of this kind, the presence of parents, family, and other guests can enhance the celebration. You might also want to invite the catechumens in your parish so they can be introduced to the assembly.

Symbols of Holy Week should be displayed in as bold a fashion as possible, including holy oils, a large, preferably crude wooden cross, the Paschal Candle, and water. Pictures and symbols of light and water should also be displayed.

Prior to the assembly, divide participants into small study groups. Ask each group to research one of the seven symbols highlighted in this service. If you don't have seven groups, some groups can take two symbols. There should be rehearsals of the 14 reading parts so that they can be proclaimed boldly, clearly, and with enthusiasm.

Time to Listen

Group One: The Blessing of Oils

Reader One: On Thursday of Holy Week, or on another designated day, the bishop and priests of the diocese will gather with parish leaders at the cathedral (the bishop's church). Three kinds of special oils will be blessed there. Some of these oils will be carried back to our own parish church.

Reader Two: They will be kept in a special display case, and used to anoint chosen people in our parish. Among these chosen people are our catechumens, our newly baptized, our newly confirmed, and our sick. All of us were

anointed at baptism with sacred oil. We are all chosen people.

(The following choral testimony can be recited by two people from group one.)

Speaker One: Oil gives life to dry skin.

Speaker Two: Sacred oil gives new life to dry spirits.

Speaker One: Oil protects the body from the burning rays of the sun.

Speaker Two: Sacred oil protects the newly baptized from the evil of sin.

Speaker One: Oil heals the wounds of sores and rashes.

Speaker Two: Sacred oil soothes and sometimes heals the sick and dying.

Speaker One: In ancient times, oil was used to anoint kings and prophets.

Speaker Two: Today, Sacred oil marks the newly baptized as daughters and sons of God.

Group Two: The Washing of Feet

Reader Three: Palestine, the land where Jesus lived, is dry and dusty. Jesus and his contemporaries wore sandals or went barefoot. Everyone had dirty feet. It was a special sign of hospitality and etiquette to give visitors water to wash their feet before they sat down to eat.

Reader Four: When Jesus gathered his friends to eat the Passover Meal, his last supper, he bent over to wash the feet of his apostles. He began with Peter. (Two participants from group two should do the following roleplay.)

Peter: Lord, are you going to wash my feet?

Jesus: Yes, you will understand why later.

Peter: You shall never wash my feet!

Jesus: If I don't, you can't share what belongs to me.

Peter: Then wash all of me, not only my feet, but my hands and head as well.

Reader Five: Jesus washed the feet of his followers as an example to us. On Holy Thursday, the priest (or other ministers) will wash the feet of twelve parishioners in imitation of Jesus. We learn from this that we should always be ready to serve others and take care of their needs.

(If possible, now have a symbolic washing of feet. Ask for volunteers beforehand, and explain how the washing will be done. Volunteers will need to know if they should wear shoes and socks, when to take them off, how you will do the washing, etc.)

Group Three: The Holy Table

(Several group members should dress the bare altar table with a table cloth, flowers, and candles.)

Reader Six: There is something very special about tables. They bring people together to share food and drink. People tell stories and share their lives when they gather around a table.

Reader Seven: The night before Jesus died, he gathered his friends around a table for what was to be his last supper with them. They remembered the good times and worried about what lay ahead. Because it was the Sabbath, they also shared the sacred stories about God's loving care for the chosen people. Jesus told them goodbyes. But not really goodbye!

Group Three: Bread and Wine

(Several from this group should bring forward to the table a loaf of unsliced bread and a carafe of wine. Have them hold up the loaf and the carafe so that participants can see them clearly as the following choral testimony is recited.)

Speaker One: Bread is made from thousands of grains of wheat.

Speaker Two: The grain is ground into flour.

Speaker One: Bread smells good when it's baking.

Speaker Two: Bread is a universal food throughout the world.

Speaker One: Wine is made from thousands of grapes.

Speaker Two: The grapes are pressed together to make juice.

Speaker One: The juice is aged until it ferments.

Speaker Two: Wine is served at celebrations.

Speaker One: At the last supper Jesus took bread, blessed it, and said:

Speaker Two: This is my body which will be given up for you.

Speaker One: Then he took a cup of wine, blessed it, and said:

Speaker Two: This cup is the cup of my blood which will be poured out for you.

Speaker One: Then Jesus said: Come together, again and again.

Speaker Two: Remember me by eating this holy bread.

Speaker One: Remember me by drinking from this holy cup.

Group Four: The Cross

Reader Eight: I invite you to close your eyes and imagine with me for a moment that we are a group of Christians living 40 years after the death and resurrection of Jesus. Bad things are happening to Christians. The Roman government has outlawed Christianity and forbidden us to assemble as a group. If we get caught, we will be arrested, put on trial, and very likely put to death.

Reader Nine: These first Christians needed a symbol to remind them that Jesus was among them, one that would help them identify themselves to each other but not to the enemy. Listen as they decide upon a symbol.

(This group of four speakers should first of all stand before the cross you have displayed and bow deeply toward it for a moment of silent prayer. Then they should roleplay the following clearly and dramatically so that the entire assembly can hear and follow their testimony.)

Speaker One: The governor's new orders say that we can no longer gather publicly.

Speaker Two: When will we share the holy bread and cup then?

Speaker Three: How will we recognize other believers?

Speaker Four: They can't stop us from gathering, we'll just meet in secret.

Speaker One: But if anyone finds out, we'll be arrested. We have to be careful!

Speaker Two: What about visitors from other towns? How will they know where to find us?

Speaker Three: I have an idea. Why don't we use a sign, something that only other Christians can understand.

Speaker Four: We could use a cross, but maybe that would be admitting defeat.

Speaker One: No, because the cross isn't only a sign of death and defeat. Jesus overcame the cross, so it's also a sign of victory.

Speaker Two: We have every right to be proud of the cross.

Speaker Three: Let's agree then that the cross will be our special sign.

Speaker Four: I wonder, will Christians cherish this sign as we do thousands of years from now?

Group Six: The Paschal (or Easter) Candle

(This group approaches the Paschal Candle and bows deeply toward it for a moment of silent prayer. One of the group members should then light it. Once it is lit, individuals in the group should do the following roleplay.)

Speaker One: This is a big candle. It is almost as tall as I am.

Speaker Two: It's big because it's important. It's the Paschal Candle.

Speaker Three: Light makes me feel happy, I hate the dark.

Speaker Four: I like the sun and the moon and the stars.

Speaker One: And I like bright lights.

Speaker Two: Jesus is like the light.

Speaker Three: He called himself the light of the world.

Speaker Four: The darkness of death couldn't hold him.

Speaker One: Now his light shines on us.

Speaker Two: It feels good to stand in the light of Jesus

Speaker Three: Easter is a time when we celebrate the light of Jesus Christ.

Group Six: Water

Reader Ten: Water is a meaningful Easter symbol of new life. The waters of baptism are blessed at the Easter Vigil and catechumens are baptized then. Babies are baptized on other Sundays of the year. Each Sunday is a "little Easter."

(Members of this group now do the following choral testimony.)

All: Water...water...water.

(Pause)

Left side: Water cleans us when we're dirty.

Right Side: It is necessary for plants to grow.

Left Side: When we're thirsty, water satisfies us.

Right Side: It refreshes us when we swim and play in it.

All: Water is a gift from God.

Reader Eleven: In the beginning God created the heavens and the earth. Now the earth was a formless void. There was darkness over the deep and God's spirit hovered over the waters. God said "Let there be a vault in the waters to divide the waters in two." And so it was.

Reader Twelve: God made the vault and divided the waters above the vault from the waters under the vault. God called the waters above the vault, heaven. God said, "Let the waters under heaven come together and let dry land appear." and so it was. God called the dry land, earth...and the huge bodies of water, sea.

Left Side: Water is a sign of power and energy.

Right Side: Water is a sign of life and nourishment.

Left Side: Water is a sign of freshness and beauty.

All: Water gives life! Baptism gives new life!

Reader Thirteen: The baptismal waters in our parish will soon be used to baptize the catechumens who are now completing their journey toward baptism. (Proclaim the names of the parish's catechumens. If you have invited them to this assembly, introduce them. Before reciting the closing prayers, encourage participants to attend the parish liturgical services on Holy Thursday, Good Friday, and Holy Saturday (the Easter Vigil).

Closing Prayer

This blessing highlights all of the sacred symbols that have been celebrated during this assembly. Announce that the response will be "We walk with you, Lord."

Leader: May the holy oil heal our spiritual wounds and seal us in our Christian faith.

All: We walk with you, Lord.

Leader: May the spiritual washing of feet remind us to serve one another.

All: We walk with you, Lord.

Leader: May the altar table remind us that we are called to the table of the Lord.

All: We walk with you, Lord.

Leader: May the bread and wine of the eucharist satisfy our spiritual hunger and thirst.

All: We walk with you, Lord.

Leader: May the cross be for us a sign of faith, victory, and new life.

All: We walk with you, Lord.

Leader: May the Easter Candle be a beacon that leads us to the light of Christ.

All: We walk with you, Lord.

Leader: May the waters of baptism refresh us, cleanse us, and give us new life.

All: We walk with you, Lord.

(Invite participants to spend several minutes in quiet, personal prayer, and then to leave the assembly area in silence.)

11
EASTER:
AN EMMAUS WALK

Background Notes

A believer comes to know Jesus as a daily companion. The derivation of the word "companion" gives important insights into practical faith. It comes from the Latin *cum* (with) and *pan* (bread) and means to share or "bread with" someone. Companions are people with whom we give and receive friendship, and with whom we share food and drink.

The companionship of Jesus is very real, but it is in the dimension of mystery and faith. Nevertheless, we can experience this presence and companionship. Traditionally, this presence has been celebrated through religious symbols, rituals, and sacraments, especially the eucharist. But it can also be experienced in the mystery of human relationships and in the events of human life.

The early followers of Jesus struggled with this mystery. How could the unseen Jesus be present? The story of the two followers on the road to Emmaus sheds light on this question and is used at the beginning of this service.

Preparation

Have ready four copies of Luke 24:13-32 in narrative form (as below). Also prepare enough copies of the "Emmaus Walk Reflection Sheet" (also as below), so that every two people can share one.

Open the assembly by asking participants to count the number present. When a total is decided upon, challenge it. Ask for a recount. Challenge the total again, and ask if anyone has figured out why you are questioning it. Explain that they did not count Jesus who is also present. As Christians we believe in the presence of the risen Christ. Invite discussion about how participants experience the companionship of Jesus in their own lives. You may find it helpful to expand upon the "Background Notes" above.

(Assign the parts of the following narrative to four of the participants. It is a dramatic adaptation of Luke 24:13-32 and should be read clearly and forcefully, with a rehearsal ahead of time.)

Time to Listen

Narrator: On that same day two of them were going to a village named Emmaus, about seven miles from Jerusalem, and they were talking to one another about all the things that had happened. As they talked and discussed, Jesus himself drew near and walked along with them; they saw him, but somehow did not recognize him. Jesus said to them,

Jesus: What are you two talking about so intently as you walk along?

Narrator: And they stood still, with sad faces. One of them, Cleopas, said to him,

Cleopas: You must be the only person living in Jerusalem who doesn't know what's been happening these last few days?

Jesus: What things?

Disciple: The things that happened to Jesus of Nazareth. This man was a prophet, mighty in words and deeds. Our chief priest and rulers handed him over to be sentenced to death, and they had him nailed to a cross. We had hoped and believed that he was the Messiah.

Cleopas: Besides all that, this is now the third day since he was crucified. Some of the women of our group went at dawn to the grave, but couldn't find his body. They came back saying they had seen a vision of angels who told them that Jesus is alive. Some of our group went to the grave and found it exactly as the women had said, but they didn't see Jesus.

Jesus: How foolish you are, how slow you are to believe everything the

prophets said! It was necessary for the Messiah to suffer these things and enter his glory.

Narrator: And Jesus explained the Scriptures to them, beginning with the books of Moses and the writings of the prophets. Then they came near Emmaus and Jesus acted as if he were going farther; but they held him back, saying,

Cleopas: Stay with us; the day is almost over and it is getting dark.

Narrator: So Jesus went in to eat with them. He sat at table with them, took the bread, and said the blessing; then he broke the bread and gave it to them. Their eyes were opened and they recognized him; but he disappeared from their sight. They said to one another,

Cleopas: Didn't we feel like a fire was burning in us when he explained the Scriptures to us?

Response

Continue now with a symbolic Emmaus walk. Invite participants to gather in pairs, and give each a copy of the "Emmaus Walk Reflection Sheet." On this sheet list the following directions:

1) Share with your partner a time that you felt abandoned by Jesus.

2) Share an experience—as you look back—when you felt the presence of Jesus very strongly. Why did you feel this way?

3) Share with one another one or more of your favorite Gospel stories.

4) Have either of you ever felt "a fire burning in you" when you heard the Scriptures explained? When and how? What would it take for you to feel this way?

Depending on weather and location, this Emmaus walk can take the form of a lengthy outing (ending with a picnic), or it can be as simple as a walk down the corridors of a building or the aisles of the church.

After the walk, have a general sharing session about the experience, and then "break bread together" by having a party (or picnic).

Note: If you plan a lengthy Emmaus walk (a full seven miles according to the Gospel story), you might also want to use this opportunity to raise money for a local charity. Participants can seek pledges of money for each mile they walk and donate the total amount to the agreed-upon cause.

12
PENTECOST: GIVING WITNESS

Background Notes

The church year reaches a climax with the Easter Vigil and it is the Easter season that this vigil ushers in. Easter is not just a single event or day, but rather a period of 50 days or seven weeks that lasts until Pentecost. It celebrates and reflects upon the abundance of graces and spiritual gifts that we have received through Christ's death and resurrection.

Pentecost (from the Greek *pentekoste*, "fiftieth"), is like a final party that celebrates the overwhelming experience of God pouring out the Spirit upon the first community of those who believed Jesus was the Lord and Christ. Pentecost is called, therefore, the birth of the church or the birth of the church's mission to the whole world.

The story of Pentecost (see Acts 2:1-4) uses very effective symbolic language to describe the excitement and enthusiasm that overwhelmed the first followers. The Spirit came "like a strong driving wind" with "tongues as of fire" that "came to rest on each of them." They responded by expressing themselves in activity and ecstasy that gave the impression of babbling and drunkenness (see 2:15). Those were exciting times and the beginning of a history of exciting times for the church.

At this time the school year is winding down. The students are looking forward to the transition to summer. This mood is incorporated in this assembly. Wonderful things are happening and it's time to give witness!

Preparation

Several weeks before this assembly, share the Pentecost story with your young people (Acts 2:1-4). Highlight the symbolic language: The Spirit came "like a strong driving wind" and "tongues as of fire came to rest on each of them." They responded by expressing themselves in activity that gave people the impression they were drunk.

This symbolic language describes a dimension of our faith that is all too often ignored: being driven and burning with enthusiasm, feeling high and excited. Highlight, therefore, the enthusiastic mission activity begun by this first band of Christians, and note that today there is a worldwide population of well over a billion Christians.

As part of your preparation, lead the group in a centering exercise that reflects upon the past school year. Ask participants to identify a group faith experience they have had with their peer group or a parish group that could be described as a Pentecost experience. What in that experience felt like "a strong driving wind" or "tongues as of fire?" Was there group enthusiasm and excitement?

Next ask each participant to identify a personal faith experience that had similar characteristics. (These experiences need not be limited to traditional religious activities. The Spirit is present in all human activities.)

After this reflection time, invite small groups of 3 or 4 to share the results of their reflection and ask one person in each group to record key experiences.

Additional preparation experiences include the following:

• Interviewing an adult about his or her religious experiences. Was there one that could be described as a Pentecost experience?

• Forming a committee to design a "Pentecost book" that contains the stories that surfaced in the small groups and the interviews with adults. This book will be used in the final assembly.

• Decorating the assembly area with mementos and souvenirs of the school year: photos, texts, awards, etc. The decorations can also include the Pentecost symbols of fire and wind.

Finally, ask two young people to rehearse the "Pentecost Experience" role-play used in this assembly (as below).

Time to Listen

The assembly continues with a solemn proclamation of a number of these group and personal Pentecost experiences.

Reader: A reading from Acts (2:1-4): When the day of Pentecost came, all the believers were gathered together in one place. Suddenly there was a noise from the sky which sounded like a strong wind blowing, and it filled the whole house where they were sitting. Then they saw what looked like tongues of fire which spread out and touched each person there. They were all filled with the Holy Spirit and began to speak in other languages, as the Spirit enabled them to speak.

This is the Word of the Lord.

All: Thanks be to God.

(If a "Pentecost book" has been constructed, have several readers share readings from it now.)

Response

("A Pentecost Experience" should now be performed by the two players. They should stand in front and hold imaginary phones.)

Martha: Don? Hi! I just got back from the weekend I told you about.

Don: You mean the one you got suckered into?

Martha: Yeah...but it really wasn't so bad. At first I thought I would just die! They assigned me to a small group of kids I thought were real losers.

Don: I told you something like that would happen.

Martha: Wait...listen. The first day was really boring. The other kids seemed to be enjoying most of it. But you know what I've been going through...with mom and dad getting divorced and all that.

Don: So, what's new? You've been grumping about that for almost a year.

Martha: And you never seem to understand. Well, anyway...for some reason I got to talking about it and how I felt. Then it just slipped out. I told them I need a hug.

Don: What were you doing talking about personal stuff? I thought weekend retreats were for talking about God and religious things. That's why I didn't go. I've had enough religion!

Martha: It just sort of fit into what we were discussing, things that were bothering us. Anyway right before the closing liturgy, we were just sitting around and talking about how we felt and someone said, "Martha never got her hug!" And before I knew it, everybody was hugging me. I never felt so good in my whole life. Then we all started hugging each other. It was the first time in a long time that I felt so good.

Don: Well, I'm glad you feel better. But it still doesn't sound like a religious weekend to me. Maybe I'll go next time!

Continue the assembly now with a sharing session. Discuss the following: How was Martha's experience a Pentecost experience? Where did the Spirit come in? Talk about ways and opportunities that all of us can experience the presence of the risen Christ and the Spirit whom he sends. Have any of the young people had such an experience recently?

Closing Prayer

Conclude with a spontaneous prayer session. Invite participants to reflect on their experiences of the past year, both the pleasant and unpleasant ones. Then, ask them to pray these aloud, using a simple litany formula. All can respond: Jesus, hear our prayer.

13
MAY:
A TESTIMONY
TO MARY

Background Notes

Many seasonal parish rituals are no longer as popular as they were years ago. One such ritual is the traditional "May Crowning." At one time it was common to have the first communion children process to a prominently positioned statue of Mary with a little girl placing a crown of flowers on the head of the statue. This procession was accompanied by Marian songs.

The following substitute for a May crowning might be celebrated as part of an end-of-year session, or it might also be celebrated with the larger parish on a weekend in May. Another option is to celebrate it on a feast of Mary, for example the Immaculate Conception or the Assumption.

Preparation

The ritual, as it unfolds here, depends upon "testimony" from a number of participants in the group. You might also want to invite parish women (youth ministers, catechists, or mothers) to do some of the testimonies. You may want to re-write the content of them if different wording seems more appropriate for your group. The content below can at least be used as a resource for discussion and as a model for the testimonies you write with your own group.

Another option would be to invite girls and women in your parish to give testimony about how Mary may have felt at the various stages of her life.

Time to Listen

Leader: Mary is very special. Christians have felt this since the first years of Christianity. She is special because she gave flesh to the mystery of God who chose to live among us. She is the Mother of Jesus and therefore the Mother of God. In her we find the best of human and spiritual qualities, ones we can certainly imitate.

Some among us will now testify to the wonder and greatness of Mary.

First Testimony: Mary, you are the mother of Jesus. The mystery of God became flesh within you. You gave birth to the one destined to be Savior and Lord. You took care of the human needs of Jesus as he grew from a baby to a young boy, and from adolescence into manhood. You did not always know where events were leading you and your child, but you were willing to believe and to struggle to find God's purpose in all that happened.

All: Mary, please help our parents as they struggle to find meaning and mystery in their lives and in the lives of their children.

Second Testimony: Mary, you were the teacher of Jesus. Under your guidance he grew in age, wisdom, and grace. He received his religious education at your knees, at your table, in your home. The wonderful human characteristics Jesus possessed he learned from you: love, concern, caring about others. So many examples he used in his preaching and teaching came from you, because he had watched you and helped you as you baked, cooked, and sewed.

All: Mary, please be close to our parents as they guide us and teach us to grow in faith.

Third Testimony: Mary, you were friend and neighbor to the people in Nazareth. What you were like in your everyday relationships is clear from what your son became and what he taught. He asked everyone to look out for the needs of others, to be concerned about their "neighbor." It was that kind of concern for others that you showed at the wedding at Cana.

All: Mary, help us be good friends and neighbors, responding to the needs of others, especially when tempted to be selfish, narrow-minded, or prejudiced.

Fourth Testimony: Mary, you were the greatest of all homemakers. Besides your day-to-day chores, you faced life's challenges in an outstanding way. You survived times of fear, for example when Herod searched for your child. When Jesus was lost in Jerusalem, you did not panic. Instead, you looked for an answer to the mystery. You stood close by when your son was being put to death. And after his death you received his body into your arms. You showed strength, courage, and a searching faith as a woman, mother, and homemaker.

All: Holy Mary, pray for us as we do our daily chores at home, and also when we face difficulties and special challenges away from home.

Fifth Testimony: Mary, you are our mother today. As Jesus hung on the cross, he gave all of us to you as your children and he gave you to us. Stay close to us in our times of need. Show yourself to us as mother, just as you did long ago to Jesus.

All: Mother Mary, pray for us. Mother Mary, protect us. Keep us close to your son, Jesus. Make us good members of your family, the church.

Response

Invite participants to write prayer responses to or about Mary in their own words. Allow ten minutes or so for this.

Closing Prayer

Use here the prayers written by the young people, and then close by praying together the Magnificat, Mary's own "proclamation" to her cousin, Elizabeth.

Right Side: My soul glorifies the Lord, and my spirit rejoices in God, my savior.

Left Side: For God has done great things for me, and holy is his name.

Right Side: From age to age God has shown mercy to those who honor him. and stretched out his mighty arm to scatter the proud.

Left Side: God has brought down the mighty from their thrones and lifted up the lowly. God has filled the hungry with good things and sent the rich away empty.

Right Side: God has remembered to show mercy to Abraham and to all his descendants forever. Amen.

14
THE SEASONS: CELEBRATING LIFE'S CYCLES

Background Notes

Positive aspects of the theme "dying" were briefly introduced in previous services for Lent and Advent. This assembly can be used at any time of the year, in any season, but it might be particularly appropriate for the transition times from fall to winter or from winter to spring.

Discuss with your young people some of the special themes and "mystery" dimensions associated with transitions. Are they aware of transitions in nature, such as the relation of earth to the sun and the tilting of our planet, which caus-

es the cycle of seasons? Seasonal transitions influence many of our liturgical customs and popular religious traditions. They are also a starting point for discussions about change, life and death, and the cycles of life in general.

Are the young people in your group comfortable with discussions about death? Unfortunately, this theme is ignored in many textbooks. Yet, young people are very curious about it. Many of them may, in fact, be preoccupied with it, even though the significant adults in their lives aren't aware of this. Indeed, almost every young person in your group will have already had numerous personal experiences of death, for example of a favorite pet, a relative, friend, or neighbor, so it is important to offer this topic for their group prayer and reflection.

Preparation

Ask some of your young people to help you decorate your assembly area with pictures and drawings of people of various ages. They might also want to display bold printings of the names of babies in the parish and of people in the parish who have died during the year.

Invite participants to discuss their personal experiences of new birth. Has there recently been a birth in their family? Have they been around a baby lately? What are some of the things they notice about babies and their reaction to the world around them?

Now ask them to discuss their personal experiences of death.

What relatives have died? How did they feel? What friends or acquaintances have died? Have they been personally involved in a funeral and burial? How did they feel? What questions do they have? (Note: Questions are often more important than answers. Be careful not to provide too many traditional answers to question about death and what comes after it. Death is probably the greatest mystery of human life, and it is precisely that: a mystery. Only faith gives answers.)

Time to Listen

Reader One: A reading from the Gospel of John (14: 18-20):
When I leave, you will not be left all alone; I will come back to you. In a little while the world will see me no more, but you will see me; and because I live, you also will live. When that day comes, you will know that I am in my Father and that you are in me, just as I am in you.

Reader Two: A second reading from the Gospel of John (11: 17-26):

When Jesus arrived, he found that Lazarus had been buried for four days. When his sister, Martha, heard that Jesus was coming, she went out to meet him. Martha said to Jesus, "If you had been here my brother would not have died. But I know that even now God will give you whatever you ask for." Jesus said to her, "I am the resurrection and the life. Whoever believes in me will live, even though they die; and whoever lives and believes in me will never die."

This is the Word of the Lord.

All: Thanks be to God.

(You might also want to ask someone to read sections from the book, *The Fall of Freddie the Leaf* by Leo Buscaglia (available from your local library). This is a beautiful story about the cycles of life and death.)

Response

Ask the young people to pray spontaneous prayers for the gift of new life given to the babies in their lives. Then ask them to pray for relatives, friends, or acquaintances who have died in the past year.

The response to these prayers should be:

All: We praise you, God for the cycles of life and death.

(After the spontaneous prayers, conclude as below.)

Closing Prayer

Leader: God, our parent, teach us to value the time you have given us in our lives to change and to grow. Thank you for those moments when we experience living to the full and understand the meaning of dying. Thank you for times of growing and waiting, of joy, and of sorrow. Show us the way to use our gifts of life more fully that we might come to our dying believing that new life with you awaits us. We ask these things in the name of Jesus who has shown us the way.

All: Amen.

15
SUNDAYS:
WHY GO TO MASS?

Background Notes

At some time in their religious formation, adolescents need to come to grips with their feelings about going to weekly Mass. Their reluctance to do so both confuses and angers many parents, although these same parents probably felt a similar reluctance when they were young. This reluctance is connected with the stages of faith that every young person goes through, one of which is a natural tendency to reject the faith and religious practices of parents.

Keep in mind that there is a difference between "rebellion" and "disengagement." Adolescents probably are not rebelling against their church when they balk at going to Mass. Rebellion is a conscious and concerted effort to tear down or to refashion ideas or institutions by force or persuasion. Many adolescents do feel rebellious, but this is usually a transitional attitude, an expression of resistance toward demands placed on them by family and school. When this rebellious attitude includes the church, it is more often than not a resistance to those in authority. Ordinarily it is not a sign of loss of faith.

Many teenagers temporarily turn their backs on religious practices. They are going through a time of religious *disengagement*. This is a normal feature of adolescence. It is a form of withdrawal from religious practices that mean little to them at this time in their lives. Many powerful physical and emotional forces are engaging their attention—making religious activities seem temporarily unimportant.

Rebellious attitudes and deliberate disengagement are features of the roleplay below. It challenges adolescents to find a place for themselves in the family of faith we call church. This roleplay deals honestly with the excuses young people frequently give. It does not put them down. Nor does it imply that their current feelings are final.

Note: This service can be used at any time of the year, in any season.

Preparation

Ahead of time, assign parts for the roleplay (as below). Although only a brief preparation is needed, it is important that the readers speak clearly and dramatically for the benefit of all participants.

Time to Listen

Reader: Believe it or not, there is a Bible story about a teenager who got bored during Mass, with severe consequences! Here's how it goes.

"On the first day of the week when they gathered to break bread, Paul spoke to them because he was leaving the next day; he kept on speaking until midnight. There were many lamps in the upstairs room where they were gathered, and a young man named Eutychus who was sitting on the window sill was sinking into a deep sleep as Paul talked on and on. Finally overcome by sleep, Eutychus slipped off the sill and fell out the third story window. When he was picked up, he was dead. Paul went down, threw himself upon him, and said as he embraced him, 'Don't be alarmed; there is life in him.' Then Paul returned upstairs, broke the bread, and ate; and, after a long conversation that lasted until daybreak, he departed. And they took Eutychus away alive and were immeasurably comforted" (Acts 20:7-12).

This is the Word of the Lord.

All: Thanks be to God.

(The five participants who will be doing the roleplay should be sitting as if in the school lunchroom. The characters are: Jason, who is very rebellious about going to church; Steve, who is not too keen about going to Mass, but is willing to be motivated; Marcie, who has answers and is confident about her own motivation for attending liturgy; Holly, who is cynical and a little bitter about almost everything; and Andy, who tends to agree with everyone. Explain the setting to participants and ask them to listen to see with whom they most identify.)

Jason: I got in a lot of trouble last Sunday because I said I didn't feel like going to church.

Steve: I know. It's the same at our house.

Marcie: Of all the things you hate to do, I bet going to Mass ranks highest.

Jason: My parents just give me stupid reasons for going. They can't even think of anything decent.

Andy: They probably don't want to. I don't think they like it that much either.

Holly: I think going to church is stupid. The music is dumb and the people are a bunch of hypocrites. They think they're so perfect just because they go to church once a week.

Steve: Nobody even smiles in church. At least we admit we don't like it.

Andy: That's probably why we have so much fun when we're together. We don't fake anything.

Holly: That's another thing wrong. My mom thinks I hang out with you guys too much. She thinks I ignore my own family.

Marcie: So, what's the problem? We've been together for years.

Andy: That's what I like about you guys. I can relax with you.

Steve: Going to school is boring, but its fun being with people you know. Not like church.

Holly: Going to church is about as bad as my chores. That's probably why they call the church a family. It's boring and you have to do things you don't like to do.

Marcie: So, why do you do your chores if you don't like to?

Holly: I have to. Like my mother says, "You live here and you have to do what I say."

Jason: My parents tell me I owe something to the family.

Andy: My dad thinks I should have more family spirit. He says that I may think my friends families are better, but they're not.

Steve: I went to a really gross family reunion last summer. I was so bored. I didn't know anybody. This guy came up to me and said he thought he was my cousin. All I said was, "So, what's so great about that?" But then we talked about cars and it wasn't so bad.

Andy: When my family gets together they talk about the "good old days." Some of it's pretty cool, but I get bored sometimes.

Marcie: Maybe that's why our parents keep going to church. It reminds them of the "good old days."

Steve: I'm getting tired of fighting about it, but I really don't get anything out of going to church.

Holly: What I want to know is who picks out those gross church songs?

Jason: I'd be willing to go if I got anything out of it, but I don't.

Steve: I hate school, too, but at least I learn something. What do you learn from church?

Andy: I can understand why our parents force us to go. That's their responsibility. They make me go to the dentist, too. I don't like that either.

Marcie: Holly, when you were talking about your family, you said you do things because you belong to the family. Jason, you said your parents make you do things because you owe it to your family.

Steve: So, you're saying that if we felt about church the same way we feel about our families, it would be a reason for going to Mass?

Marcie: Maybe. It would be okay if we felt the same way about church as we do about our families. I think we will someday.

Holly: So what does the church expect of me? To put money in the collection, or to volunteer for something, or what?

Marcie: I'm not sure, but we keep saying we don't get anything out of church. Maybe we can't as long as we go with a negative attitude.

Jason: So how can we be positive if we don't even want to be there? Wouldn't it be funny if no one showed up at Mass some Sunday?

Marcie: Well, in a way it would be awful. Somehow you just depend on other people to keep on praying, even if we don't want to. We need them to keep believing in God and to keep on worshiping God.

Andy: I think I know what you mean. The people at church are our family. And we need them. Maybe they need us, too. Just like with any family.

Marcie: I'll be honest. I've done my share of complaining about church. There was a time when I refused to go. But now I go because I want to...and need to. I go for a reason. Call it God. Call it family. I need to go. So I go.

Jason: Hold on. You keep talking about church as a family. I was never asked to be a part of it.

Holly: You didn't ask to be part of your family at home either. Your parents got you into both families.

Jason: I never had a choice. I don't feel like I belong to either family.

Holly: Our parents get us baptized when we can't do anything about it. And then they dump this whole church thing on us!

Jason: Right!

Marcie: Steve, what you said about your family reunion, I bet deep down you're really proud of your family. And you just don't want to admit it. I bet you other guys are really proud of our church. And, like Steve, you're just afraid to admit it.

Jason: So you're saying I belong to that old lady that sits in the pew in front of me every Sunday. I don't even know her name. I don't even know what she looks like.

Steve: So whose fault is that? Next time you go to church, poke her and ask.

Andy: We've spent all this time talking about church. So how come no one has mentioned God? I think that's kind of funny.

Marcie: That's not funny. When was the last time we brought God into anything?

Jason: I don't believe in God. Nothing has proven to me that God exists. Why should I waste my time on going to church?

Steve: That's not the way I feel. In fact, God is the main reason I go to church.

I figure God wants to see me around once in a while.

Holly: This is beginning to sound like religion class. Let's drop the subject. It's getting too personal.

Marcie: Well, we've been friends so long, what's wrong with talking about personal things?

Holly: So, I'm supposed to get all excited about church and God because you do?

Marcie: That's not a bad idea. After all, God is the reason we go to church. I don't have all the answers, but I'm willing to look for them.

Steve: I think the problem is we don't know what's going on when we go to church.

Marcie: Is it that we don't know what's going on, or is it that we don't care?

Andy: I think it's both. One comes from the other. We don't know what's going on, so we don't care. I guess I do want to get more involved. But I don't know how.

Jason: I wouldn't mind going to church if I could sit with you guys.

Holly: So, is there a law against that?

Response
After the roleplay divide participants into groups of three or four. Have them discuss the roleplay and ask them to answer these questions:
• Which character did you relate

to most? Why?

- What kind of battles go on in your homes about this?
- What do you know about the Mass right now?
- What would you want to learn about the Mass in future sessions?

Invite the small groups to report their responses to the larger group.

Closing Prayer

Leader: Lord Jesus, present here with us, teach us how to pray.

Teach us to open our minds and hearts to your Word at Mass.

Teach us to understand your presence there in the gifts of bread and wine, and to want to be there "in memory of you." Help us grow in love for you and for the Mass. We ask these things in the name of the Father and of the Son and of the Holy Spirit.

All: Amen.

16
ALL YEAR: SHARING OUR BURDENS

Background Notes

No Christian symbol is more visible or speaks more clearly than the cross. It preserves the fundamental belief of Christianity that though Jesus died on the cross, he was victoriously raised up to new life in God. Because he accepted the cross, he teaches us, his followers, that we, too, must carry it and be raised up from it as he was. The cross is, therefore, a sign of victory for us, even though it was an instrument of execution at the time of Jesus.

The cross has become a symbol of the personal burdens that we, like Jesus, must carry in life. Going beyond personal spirituality, the cross is also a symbol of the burdens carried by others that we, as Christians, are challenged to share. Jesus identified himself with the burdens of others, and he challenges us, his followers, to share those burdens, too. This is the Gospel challenge. This is Gospel morality.

Celebrate this service any time of year, in any season. It might be especially appropriate during Lent, but would also be meaningful during those times when someone in your group is carrying a particularly heavy "cross."

Preparation

During the weeks prior to this assembly, invite your young people to bring pictures and/or newspaper clippings and headlines that show the realities of poverty and suffering. Attach these to a large but simple wooden cross, and display this in a prominent place, where all can see it. This cross will be the focal point of the following service.

Time to Listen

Reader One: "The way we came to know love was that he laid down his life for us; so we ought to lay down our lives for our brothers and sisters. If someone who has worldly means sees a brother or sister in need and refuses them compassion, how can the love of God remain in that person? Children, let us love not in word or speech but in deed and truth" (John 3:16-18).

Reader Two: "Those who want to come after me, must deny themselves and take up the cross daily and follow me" (Luke 9:23).

Response

Leader: The cross that people carry is the cross of Jesus. In his parables, Jesus clearly identifies himself with the needy. The cross Jesus asks us to carry is, therefore, a blending of our own sufferings and those of others. (Point out examples from the pictures fastened to the cross. Explain that in the following meditation, you will be hearing brief descriptions of the kinds of crosses people carry.)

Leader: (facing the cross) This cross of Jesus is also the cross of lonely people who have no family or friends. They have no one to turn to, no one to walk through life with.

Leader: Are you ready to accept this cross?

All: We are ready!

Leader: Are you willing to share its burden?

All: We are willing. You can pass the cross to us!
(Ask two volunteers to move the cross a short distance closer to participants. Pause for silent prayer.)

Leader: This is the cross of hungry men and women, boys and girls, who are dying because they do not have enough to eat.

Leader: Are you ready to accept this cross?

All: We are ready!

Leader: Are you willing to share its burden?

All: We are willing. You can pass the cross to us!
(Have the cross moved still closer to participants. Pause for prayer.)

Leader: This is the cross of sick people who are suffering because they have no doctors, medicine, or hospitals. They have no money to pay for special care.

Leader: Are you ready to accept this cross?

All: We are ready!

Leader: Are you willing to share its burden?

All: We are willing. You can pass the cross to us!
(Now have the cross go into the midst of participants. Pause for prayer.)

Leader: This is the cross of addicted people, who must have drugs and alcohol to survive. They need help to free themselves from their addictions.

Leader: Are you ready to accept this cross?

All: We are ready!

Leader: Are you willing to share it?

All: We are willing. You can pass the cross to us!
(Move the cross farther into the group. Pause for prayer.)

Leader: This is the cross of people who are physically handicapped. They cannot live and move freely in our society. They can't enjoy the world around them as we can.

Leader: Are you ready to accept this cross?

All: We are ready!

Leader: Are you willing to share it?

All: We are willing. You can pass the cross to us!
(Move the cross farther yet into the group. Pause for prayer.)

Leader: This is the cross of people who are emotionally handicapped. They are afraid to live life to the full. They are hesitant and alone.

Leader: Are you ready to accept this cross?

All: We are ready?

Leader: Are you willing to share it?

All: We are willing. You can pass the cross to us!
(Move the cross yet again. Pause for prayer.)

Leader: This is the cross of people in our families and in our parish who are suffering right now. This is the cross of those among us in this room who are suffering.

Leader: Are you ready to accept this cross?

All: We are ready!

Leader: Are you willing to share it?

All: We are willing. You can pass the cross to us!
(The cross should now be carried back to the front of the assembly. Pause for prayer.)

Leader: (facing the cross) This is the cross of Jesus. It is heavy with the sufferings of all people down through the ages. Let us pray now, each in his or her own heart, for the courage to accept the cross and share the burdens of others, as Jesus did. (Pause for silent prayer and reflection.)

Closing Prayer
Leader: Jesus, our friend and leader, teach us how to reach out to others and help them carry the burdens life places on them. Help us, too, to carry our own burdens with your help. We ask these things in the name of the Father and of the Son and of the Holy Spirit.

All: Amen.